INDIAN BASKETS

Close-up reveals one of many Indian art forms that
consistently appears as a symbol of their culture.

INDIAN BASKETS

OF THE NORTHWEST COAST

BY ALLAN LOBB

PHOTOGRAPHY BY ART WOLFE

DRAWINGS BY BARBARA PAXSON

International Standard Book Number, Regular Edition 0-912856-37-8
International Standard Book Number, Deluxe Edition 0-912856-44-0
Library of Congress Catalog Number 78-51216
Copyright© 1978 by Graphic Arts Center Publishing Co.
2000 N.W. Wilson · Portland, Oregon 97209 · 503/224-7777
Publisher · Charles H. Belding
Designer · Robert Reynolds
Printer · Graphic Arts Center
Binding · Lincoln & Allen
Printed in the United States of America

This basket collection occured
largely as a result of the friend-
ship and help of Laurence Tyler,
and the book as a result of the
interest and effort of Marlene
Dorsett and John Pollock.

INTRODUCTION

Those of us who live in the Pacific Northwest have the advantage and pleasure of being able to relate to and envision our entire known past. We are near in time to the remnants of a great culture, the residuals of which closely touched the lives of our parents and grandparents.

Archaeological finds show that the native peoples have a heritage which extends back thousands of years, yet what we know of them is of comparatively recent origin. They developed one of the richest cultures in North America, but, like many other peoples, left no written histories.

Our first records about the Indians of the Northwest Coast and their ways of life are to be found in journals of the Russian, Spanish and English explorers of the late 18th century and in writings of a few fur traders and travelers.

Even today, the sites visited by the early explorers, traders and trappers have not greatly changed. We can travel along the coastline from the Columbia River between Oregon and Washington to southern Alaska and recreate an image of the dwelling places and sources of livelihood unique to the native peoples. We can locate the sites of villages along rivers, streams, and lakes, many of which bear the Indian names.

A short motor trip can take us to places where we can envision the canoes, encampments and smoke from the fires of the peoples who named the Quinault, the Cowlitz, the Nisqually, the Skagit and the Nooksack.

A day's trip north from Puget Sound brings us to the Fraser River and to settings which may prompt visions of the beautiful art of the Thompson, the Lillooet, or the Chilcotin tribes which lived in the inland valleys.

The inlets along the coast and the islands wooded with giant cedars and towering spruce and thick with ferns and great varieties of plants remind us of a culture which created baskets of such quality and beauty that they are now studied and appreciated the world over as an art form.

Anthropologists have observed and documented elements of basketry over most of the world and over virtually all of North America, with some of the finest examples being those by Indians of the Northwest Coast. (Within this book, the term Northwest Coast includes the western portions of the States of Oregon and Washington, the Province of British Columbia, the southern coast and extremity of Alaska and the Aleutian Islands.) The ravages of nature are rapidly destructive of natural fiber materials, particularly in the damp regions of the Pacific Northwest, so that only a few remnants of early weaving and basketry have been discovered here.

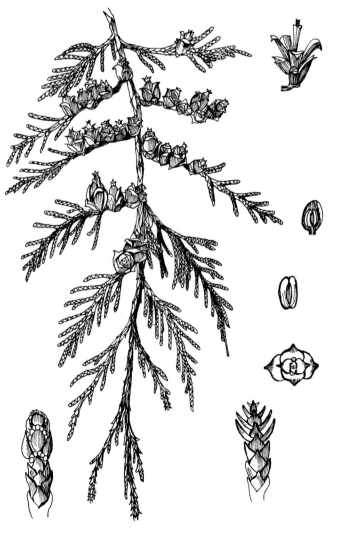

Cedar (Thuja plicata)

The oldest human remains found in North America are about 10,000 years old. Excavations at the Marme Rock shelter in southeastern Washington presented an important source for such material. At that time the region at The Dalles on the Columbia River had been settled. Artifacts from the Fraser River Canyon in British Columbia support evidence of human habitation approximately 9,000 years before our time.

Artifacts similar to those of the Fraser and Columbia valleys were used by the earliest occupants of the Puget Sound region, the Fraser River delta country, and the Gulf of Georgia. Finds of items approximately 3,000 years old include stone fish net sinkers, harpoon points, primitive fish knives, bone needles and awls for basketry.

Specimens of crudely woven basketry of the Locarno Beach phase of pre-history (1000 to 500 B.C.), have been found in British Columbia. These included the wrapped crossed warp weave using split cedar roots and branches.

Northwest Indian culture dating back 2,000 years is being studied at excavations of the abandoned Ozette Indian Village of the Makah on the Pacific Coast of the Olympic Peninsula. This site, which had been covered by mud slides, has most recently revealed the structure and contents of a 300-500-year-old household. Building style, hunting implements and household receptacles are closely related to artifacts collected in the 18th and 19th centuries. Remnants of basketry display techniques unique to this area of the Northwest coast.

Farther north, caves on the Aleutian Islands have preserved and yielded evidence of prehistoric basketry and mat weaving. The exceedingly fine workmanship is similar to that for which the modern Aleut is famous. The twined weave with false embroidery is a technique which is identical to that used by the Tlingit.

TECHNIQUES

There are many basketry techniques, along with variations in application and decoration. Some of the techniques were used by most of the Indians of the Northwest and others were indigenous to a smaller region.

Baskets are either handwoven or sewn. Sewn basketry is generally refered to as "*coiled.*"

The basic structure of all woven baskets makes use of horizontal elements called the *weft* (sometimes referred to as *woof)* and vertical elements called the *warp.*

Handweaving is of several types: plaiting (checker work, twilled work, wicker work); twining and wrapping.

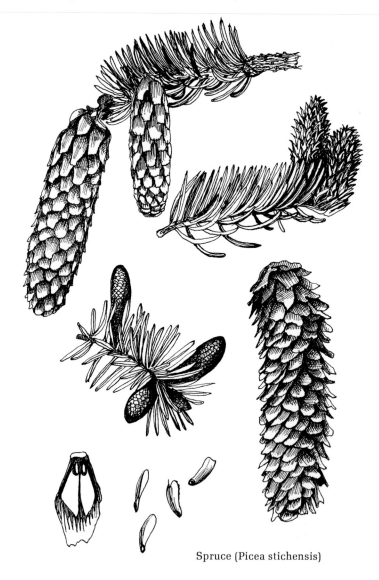

Spruce (Picea stichensis)

6

Plaiting

Checker work is a technique using a warp and weft of the same width, thickness and pliability; weaving the weft strand in and out, over one warp strand and under the next. Checker work was done by most of the Indians of the Northwest Coast. We associate it with the wallets and the basket boxes of the Tsimshian, Bella Bella and Nootka and with the Indians of the Puget Sound basin. It is used consistently in the bottoms of baskets of the Makah and the Nootka, and its use in matting is fairly universal. It is not possible to tell from looking at the bottom of the baskets and at the matting of British Columbia and Puget Sound Indians which is warp and which is weft.

Twilled work is a variation of checker work in which each element of the weft is passed over and under two or more warp elements, thus producing a diagonal or twilled pattern. Decorative effects were created through the use of two or more colored materials. The technique was quite common in British Columbia among the Haida and in Washington State. The Clallam Indians on the Strait of Juan de Fuca were perhaps the first to produce the twilled weave.

Wicker work differs from checker work in that either the warp or the weft—but not both—is rigid. Examples of this style of weaving may sometimes be seen in the bottom of some Indian baskets.

Twining, which has several types, was used along the entire Pacific Coast, from California to Alaska, where the Aleut produced such elegant weaving that examples have the quality of fine linen fabric. Twined work has two or more weft strands which are twisted or twined in half turns on each other as they weave in and out between the warps. Twining adapts well to the weaving of open work as well as closed work baskets.

Plain closed twined weaving can be perfectly watertight and is the standard weave of the majority of all woven baskets. It consists of the simple twining of two weft strands around each successive warp element with the weft driven down. The regular weave produces the vertical ridge-like appearance on the line of the warp, the exterior surface of the weft forming the outside or ornamental base of the work. Its finest application was by the Tlingit, Aleut and Haida.

Open twined weaving has open space or separation between the rows of weaving or twining. The warp strands are parallel.

A combined twined and checker weave involves the introduction of a single weft strand in checker or wicker weaving in between the lines of the regular twining. It may be used to

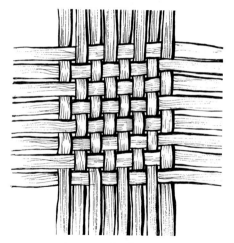

Plaiting—checker weave

Plaiting—twilled weave

save material; there is, however, a loss of strength, rigidity and closeness of the texture.

Diagonal twined weaving differs from the plain in that the wefts cross over two or more warp elements at each turn, so that the ridges on the outside surface are not vertical as in plain twining but are diagonal. This weave produces the ornamentation of the Haida hat rim and the Haida basket marginal pattern, as well as variations in Tlingit decoration.

Crossed warp twining makes use of two sets of warp elements, one set inclining to the right and the other to the left. The twining binds the two together, forming a decorative mesh. The Aleut were adept in the use of other double warp combinations, both separating and diverting the two elements of the double warp in open twining.

Three-strand twined weaving makes use of three weft strands instead of two. Each weft passes over two warp strands externally and under one warp on the inside of the basket. A diagonal, rope-like appearance is produced on the outside of the basket. This is a strong weave. On the inside, there is no appearance of ornament. Variations include a three-strand braid and a three-strand embroidery as used by the Tlingit.

Coiled basketry is sometimes called *sewn* because a needle, usually a bone awl, and threads of flexible materials are used to fasten the coils and form the basket. The foundation of the coil may be a single element such as a stem or rod, two stems or other elements side by side, several splints or small stems, lengths of grass or shreds of other materials, wrapped into bundles. The coils, unlike the vertical warp in twining, spiral around the basket horizontally. The stitches pass around the foundation also in a continuous spiral, each stitch interlocking or bifurcating the one immediately beneath it or passing through the coil underneath.

Coiled basketry in all areas was made using a variety of techniques. There were bottoms with round watchspring, elongated watchspring or parallel coiling, and others with a slat or flat pieces of wood wrapped or bound variously. Side walls varied with the size of the coil, and with the different degrees of flatness, depending on the type of material used. Rims might be braided or wrapped. Types of loop work and the use of lids varied within and among the tribes.

Wrapping

A weave heretofore referred to as wrapped twining may more accurately be called a wrapped crossed warp weave. One warp strand is placed horizontally crossing a vertical warp

Diagonal twined weaving

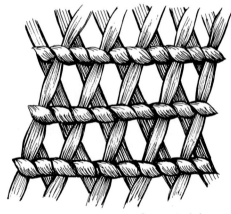

Crossed warp twining

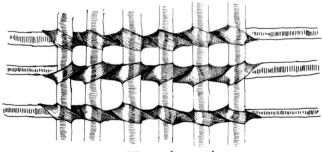

Wrapped crossed warp
"birdcage weave"

element, usually on the inside of the basket, forming a lattice. The third element, more flexible, a weft strand, is wrapped around the crossing of the horizontal and the vertical warp elements. On the outside of the basket, the turns of the wrapping are oblique; on the inside, they are vertical. When the weaving is beaten home, the surface is not unlike that of a tiled roof, the wrapping of the weft overlying each other with perfect regularity. This style of weaving was introduced by the Nootkan peoples, including the Makah and Clallam. Examples of wrapped crossed warp weaving sometimes called *birdcage twining,* are seen in the soft hats and wallets of Salish Indian tribes, the Nez Perce and the Klickitat. In this work, they used soft material for the warp elements and the wrapping weft.

The *Clam basket* exemplifies this technique with spacing between the warp elements forming a fairly open latticework.

Base, coiled basket—watch spring coiling

ORNAMENTATION

The Indian women who were the basketmakers of the Northwest Coast enhanced their work with a variety of methods of ornamentation. Rims or edges of baskets were braided or a coil added and loops or scallops worked on. Decorative effects were achieved by varying the weaves within a basket, using the combining close twining and open work or checker work or skip stitch. Painting was used on the hats of the Haida, Tlingit, Kwakiutl, and Nootka. Various methods and materials were used to overlay a decorative design.

False embroidery, which was not done with a needle, was a favorite method of creating patterns or designs on twined baskets. As the weaver proceeded, she wrapped the decorative strand once around each external structural strand of the weft as it crossed the warp. The wrappings of false embroidery look like twining on the finished basket, but slant in opposite direction to the twining wefts. The false embroidery does not appear on the inside of the basket.

An *overlay* was also used in twined weaving using a "double weft". A contrasting color is placed on top of the element to be twined, and is carried along with it. If only one of the twining elements or weft structures is so covered or doubled, the resulting design will show only every other stitch with the added color, but if both are covered, continuous lines of color are achieved and elaborate designs may be worked.

Imbrication was a method of overlay ornamentation unique to Indians in parts of British Columbia on the Fraser River, in southwest Canada, on the upper waters of the Columbia and in many Salishan tribes of western Washington. The

Overlay—false embroidery over plain twining

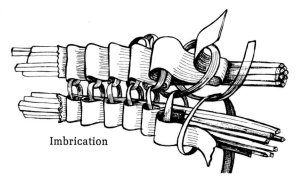

Imbrication

9

strip of colored bark or grass is laid down along the coil and caught under a passing or encircling stitch. Before another stitch is taken, this one is bent forward to cover the last stitch, doubled backward on itself so as to be underneath the next stitch. So, with each one, it is bent backward and forward so that the sewing is concealed entirely except for the exposed external element. A variation includes covering alternate stitches only.

Beading is the application of an overlay decorative element over the outside surface of a coil, using a thin strip of bark or grass or both. One or more narrow strips may be used on the same coil. The appearance is that of a ribbon drawn along the coil. The strip may pass over or under one or more stitches.

MATERIALS

The Indian women gather their material for baskets from many sources, primarily from the regions in which they lived, although there was occasional trading with Indians of other areas for desirable grasses for ornamentation.

Foundation or structural materials included rye grass, roots and limbs from young spruce and cedar, shreds of bark from cedar and birch, bast or inner bark of cedar, young shoots of hazelnut and willow, juniper roots, cattail, rush and tule stalks.

Decorative materials included rye grass, bear or squaw grass, brome grass, reeds, maize, maidenhair fern, horsetail, bark of cherry, cedar and birch, and inner bark of cedar.

The roots and limbs were peeled, then split into strands or splints. Many of the grasses were split into fibers almost as fine as thread. After the materials were split or shredded into the desired width, they would be sorted according to size, variety and length and stored. Soaking the materials in water for periods was essential in preparing them and making them pliable for use.

Color was provided by natural materials and through the use of dyes. White or cream came from the stems or leaves of shore grass, bear grass, bromegrass, hair grass and the bast of cedar.

Dark purple or black came from strips split from the surface of the roots of horsetail or scouring rush. Black also was supplied by the stems of maidenhair fern.

The bark of the wild cherry was rubbed to a glossy red.

Brown was the natural color of many basket materials.

The white or light-colored materials were darkened or made black by soaking in mud or charcoal or given new colors with dyes. A yellow dye was made by boiling or steeping the twigs

Overlay—Imbrication over coiling (after Mason)

and bark of Oregon grape or wolf moss. A strong solution of dye from willow bark would provide brown and a weaker solution, yellow. Red dye came from alder bark. Juice of huckleberries was sometimes used as a purple dye.

Colored yarns and silks were often used after the Indians had been reached by the Russians and other trappers and traders.

ALEUT

Some of the finest basketry in the world was produced by the native women of the desolate, treeless, storm-swept Aleutian Islands. The women showed extaordinary skill in using a variety of twined weaving techniques to make the small, tightly-woven baskets for which they are famous. These baskets were made of slender strips of rye grass, some as fine as silk. The Aleut women split the fibers with their fingernails, which they allowed to grow long for this purpose. In later times, after their contact with the Russians (Bering discovered the islands in 1745), they wove in threads of colored silk or worsted for decorative effect.

Many kinds of grass mats, bags and baskets were woven. Mats were made for a variety of uses, such as bed coverings, screens and kayak seats. Circular utility bags and baskets were used for carrying fish and meat and as receptacles for many other purposes. These may or may not have had an open braid rim construction.

Examples of the finely-woven, delicately-decorated basket with the equally delicately-woven lid and its small, central nob or handle (many of which were done in the earlier years of the 20th century) are now held as prized possessions by many a basket collector and museum.

ALASKAN ESKIMO

Baskets generally associated with the Alaskan Eskimo are of the coiled variety. Best known are of a ginger jar configuration with a lid and knob-like central handle of the same coiled weaving. These containers were principally composed of rye grass bundle foundation, wrapped and stitched together with leaves of the same grass. The Eskimo women basketmakers employed an awl made of a bird's bone ground to a point. Baskets of a shape similar to that of an uncovered bandbox were also made. In earlier times, a bit of leather was used as the bottom to which the first coils were stitched.

In Alaska a technique of a single rod foundation coiled basketry is most in evidence amongst the Athabascan Indian tribes of the interior. Split stems of willow embrace a single willow rod foundation binding it to the coil beneath. This type

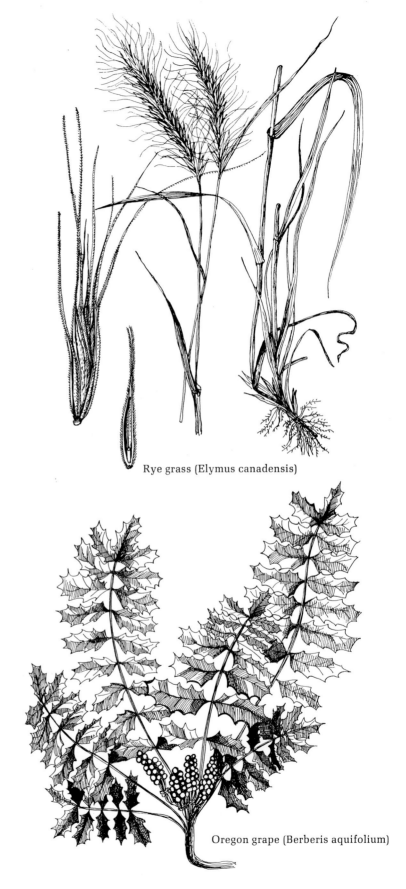

Rye grass (Elymus canadensis)

Oregon grape (Berberis aquifolium)

of coiling was also used in sewing the black or grey, usually covered, and ivory-decorated small baleen trinket or storage baskets of the North Coast Eskimo. They used finely divided strips of the baleen of whale over a single rod of the same material.

Twined basketry was also produced in the Norton Sound area and elsewhere, though it was far less refined than that of the Aleut and not to be compared with that of the Tlingit.

TLINGIT

Tlingit country, or southeastern Alaska, comprises the area between the Dixon entrance and the Copper River. This area embraces the thousands of islands called the Alexander Archipelago by the Russians.

The basket work of the Tlingit Indian is superb, both in workmanship and ornamentation. Material split from young, tough spruce root was used in either the natural color or dyed brown or black to produce finely woven pieces, with very thin walls, from watertight cooking vessels to tiny trinket containers and baskets with a capacity of a bushel or more.

The Tlingit used several styles of twined weaving. The bottom of a basket is woven, plain, in the color of the material. In many pieces, a row of checker weaving alternates with twined weaving. In building up baskets, bands of plain color, red and black are woven into the structure so that the same color appears on both the internal and external surfaces of the walls or sides, participating in the basket decoration.

The method called *false embroidery* was used to create patterns or designs and geometric configurations with color. Materials used in false embroidery were stems of a variety of grasses as well as the stems of the maiden hair fern.

The Tlingit are known for their baskets with *rattle-top* lids. In weaving the lids they would skillfully construct a hiding place for some loose pebbles. Perhaps the rattle of the pebbles would serve as an alarm if someone were trying to get into the basket.

Ceremonial hats were also woven and then painted with stylized animal designs.

HAIDA

The Haida Indians lived in the Queen Charlotte Islands. At one time, small groups also pushed northward into Tlingit country on Prince of Wales Island.

Their work was primarily in plain twined weaving with material from spruce root. Their basic basket weave was not unlike that of the Aleut and the Tlingit. However, the Haida did not finish their baskets with false embroidery or embroider with fabric.

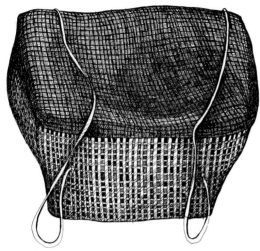

Bella Coola
Storage basket, cedar root and bark;
wrapped crossed warp. Lid, cedar bark; checker weave

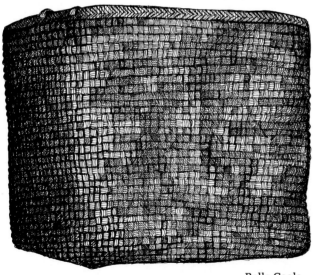

Bella Coola
Cedar bark; checker weave

Classically, the Haida basket was circled by black bands of mud-dyed spruce root. The band appeared on the inside as well as on the outside of the basket. The baskets were tightly woven and could be waterproof.

Variations in the design about the upper portion or margin of the basket were produced through use of a skip stitch or three-strand twined work.

In addition to the tightly twined weave, the Haida also used twined open work.

Unique to the Haida were twined waterproof hats with double thicknesses, and a design in the weaving, similar to that used along the margins of the baskets. These were painted traditionally in the style of decorative art of the Indians of the North Pacific Coast, with the designs colored in red and black.

TSIMSHIAN

The people along the Nass and Skeena Rivers in British Columbia produced baskets from root materials using techniques of twining, checker work and twilling.

Available specimens most frequently show the use of cedar in the production of flexible woven checker work. Baskets in this region were often rectangular, with square corners and rectangular openings.

An abundance of the bast (inner bark fibers) of the cedar and its pliable nature after suitable preparation seem to have led to checker weaving with its use in numerous types of mats, wallets and decorated baskets.

Ornamentation on these mats and baskets was introduced using different colored strands of cedar and by variation in the width and/or thickness of the warp and weft strands.

Cedar mats of varying size played an important role in the daily life of the Indians of this region. They were used for floor coverings, sleeping facilities, doors and openings for houses, as well as for boat sails and wrappings for their dead.

NOOTKA, MAKAH, KWAKIUTL

These Wakashan tribes produced cedar bark checker matting. Their checker and twilled baskets were quite common throughout western British Columbia and Washington.

The Makah and the Nootka are recognized for their introduction of the unique style of basketry referred to as wrapped crossed warp or the *birdcage* or *fish-trap* style.

The bottom of the Makah or Nootka basket classically presents a square of checker-woven cedar bark. The decussations (intersections) of each bark strand are embraced by additional rows of twined sedge grass which extend to the periphery of the bottom. The warp material is almost universally cedar

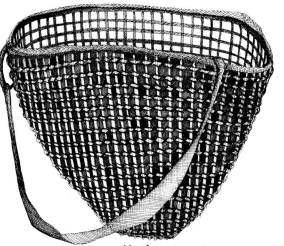

Northwest coast
cedar and spruce root
"clam basket" with tump line;
wrapped crossed warp

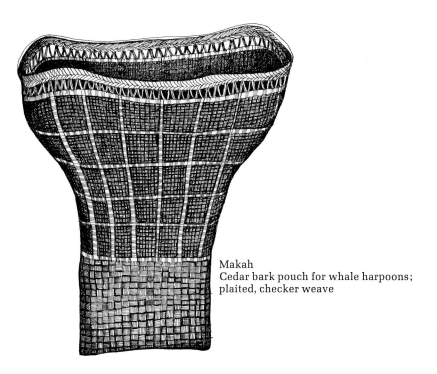

Makah
Cedar bark pouch for whale harpoons;
plaited, checker weave

13

Nootka
Cedar bark, bear grass;
wrapped crossed warp

Nootka
Cedar bark, bear grass, sedge;
wrapped crossed warp

Makah
"Clam basket"
cedar root and boughs;
wrapped crossed warp

bark, with wrapping of bear grass. The latter may be variously colored to form designs on the walls or lid of the basket. These may depict a whaling scene, with boat, hunters and whale; animal and bird forms; or geometric designs.

The classic Nootka hat described by many explorers and traders and initially collected by Captain Cook was of the same materials with a similar decorative pattern. The overlay weaving technique was used in these hats, with the double weft strand (grass on cedar) forming a basic white background against which appear dark colored figures made by reversing or twisting the double-colored weft element. Other hats were also made using a plain twined weave, with or without an overlay or painting.

The Kwakiutl used a variation of wrapped and twining technique, often with crossed warps; their work, however, was generally not as fine as that of the Makah and the Nootka.

Some of the finest work of the Kwakiutl was done in a form of checker or twilled weaving for mats, bedding, pillow bags and sacks in which dry salmon and herring roe were kept.

Among these people, transportation of goods by land was done entirely by means of carrying baskets of wrapped crossed warp or birdcage weaving. There were two main kinds, a large basket which is carried on the back and a small basket which is carried in the hand. For the large basket a wide tumpline woven of cedar bark was attached to help in carrying. Baskets for carrying and picking berries were somewhat finer and of smaller weave, while those used for carrying clams were larger, more open and coarser. The bottoms of these baskets were rounded.

THOMPSON, LILLOOET, CHILCOTIN

The Salish tribes of British Columbia were noted for their manufacture of coiled basketry. These tribes include the Lillooet, the upper and lower Thompson and the Shuswap. Of the Athabascan group of southern British Columbia, the Chilcotin were the only people who made coiled basketry. Their coiled work influenced many peoples in surrounding areas.

The cedar tree, principally the roots, furnished the greater part of material used in the manufacture of coiled baskets. When the long, pliable roots of the cedar were not available, the roots of the spruce or juniper were used for the foundation and sewing material for the coil. For the bottom, where slats of wood frequently took the place of coil, the sapwood of the cedar, or any wood easily and smoothly split, was used.

A distinctive element of coiled basketry was the decorative

component called *imbrication*. Another form of decoration was *beading*. At times both imbrication and beading were combined.

The decoration required materials more pliable than the tough roots, so the Indians gathered grasses and reeds and the bark of cherry and birch trees.

Coiled basketry in all areas was made using a variety of techniques. These were parallel, watchspring and round coiled bottoms, as well as slat bottoms. Side walls varied with the size of the coil and degrees of flatness, depending on the type of material used. Rims were made by wrapping the marginal coil and, less often, with braiding. Types of loop work and the use of lids varied within and among tribes.

The forms and purposes of such baskets included burden baskets of varying shape and size; round baskets used for basins, pails, bowls and kettles; nut- and pot-shaped baskets used to store special objects; and storage baskets.

There were large, oblong baskets with lids used for storing food and clothing. Smaller storage baskets served for holding sewing materials and trinkets. The lids were occasionally hinged to the baskets or were made to slide into place on a leather thong which served also as a handle.

Nut-shaped baskets were used in early times for holding water. Round, open baskets served as kettles, the food being boiled by throwing hot stones into water-containing baskets.

A type of basket which has a flat back made to hang against a post or wall was shaped similar to the fish basket or creel of modern times. Such baskets were used for holding tobacco and pipes. A hole in the center of the lid allowed the pipe stem to protrude.

Baby carriers of coiled basketry were, according to some sources, adopted by the Thompson from the lower Lillooet, who made them of rather narrow, flat coils or slats of cedar wood. Some were made of round coils throughout, some of a flat coil, and some of a combination of round and flat coils. The ornamentation was usually imbrication and or beading with a variation in pattern depending on the side carried against the mother's body. The carriers may have been partially covered and lined with pieces of colored cloth, and sometimes decorated with shells or other small articles which jingled.

The burden baskets of the Thompson were generally rectangular in shape, with corners somewhat rounded, the sides longer than the ends, with flaring walls from base to wide mouth, the width of the top at least double that of the base.

By comparison, the Lillooet coiled baskets are more nearly

Chilcotin, British Columbia
Burden basket
cedar root, rush, cherry bark;
imbricated

15

square, with very small bases, wide mouths, straight walls and sharp corners. In general, the Thompson coils are finer than those of the Lillooet and very uniform. The Lillooet, in many instances, used a broader, flatter coil, which is sewn with coarser materials.

The typical Chilcotin basket is somewhat smaller than the Thompson and is a little longer in proportion to its width, which gives it a deeper appearance than either the Thompson or Lillooet type. The corners are rounded.

The rim is usually much higher at the ends of the basket than on the long side, where it dips gradually toward the center and imparts to the upper section the outlines of a boat. On the outside, some distance below the rim margin, is a thick rod or wire which encircles the basket and is fastened to it by means of thongs. This rod serves as a handle to which to tie the carrying straps to lift the basket when loaded, as well as for general support. The coil of the Chilcotin is smaller and less even than those of the Lillooet or the Thompson. Classically the Thompson, Lillooet and Chilcotin burden baskets are partially imbricated or beaded with reed, rushes and cherry bark. The Thompson were patterned with "droppers" and other designs, the Lillooet with a solid imbrication or beading over the upper two-thirds of the basket and the Chilcotin consistently patterned with four horizontal imbricated design fields. The pattern might vary on the front and back side of the Thompson and Lillooet baskets depending on which side is carried against the carrier.

LOWER FRASER (STALO)

Coast Salish Indians living along the lower 105 miles of the Fraser River were divided into a number of groups or tribes, each of which claimed a stretch of river bank or an important tributary of the Fraser. The collective name which has most often been applied, and the name the natives themselves prefer, is Stalo.

Early informants state that the Stalo always made coiled, imbricated baskets of cedar roots. There were two types: the flat core of cedar slats and the round core of cedar root splints. In early times, it is said, the baskets all were of the round foundation, like the Thompson. There were large storage baskets, which held clothing and valuables; all sizes of burden baskets, which were watertight and usually made with round coils; and baskets of varying sizes, including work baskets and cradles.

In later years, the flat-core, coiled, less-tightly woven, not waterproof, not well-imbricated baskets were made by the

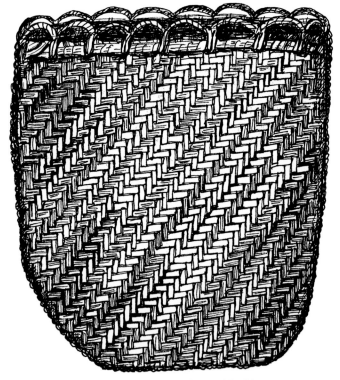

Northwest Washington
Cedar bark; twilled weave

Indians for sale and trade. It is these baskets which tend to be associated with the lower Fraser region. They obviously reflect the influence of the Thompson and the Lillooet, the latter more so toward the coast and the Straight of Georgia.

YAKIMA, KLICKITAT, NEZ PERCE

The habitat of these Indians was along the waters of the Columbia River and its tributaries, from the Cascade mountains on the west to the Bitterroot range on the east, or what is now eastern Washington and northern Idaho.

The Yakima and the Klickitat made coiled baskets of great beauty and excellent workmanship. The foundation or coils were of the roots of young cedar trees.

In general, the imbrication or ornamentation of the baskets, was done in white, brown, black and yellow, using principally cedar bark, bear grass or willow bark, and horsetail, with the occasional use of fabric. A few coiled baskets were not imbricated; others were ornamented only with beading.

The designs used by the Klickitat and the Yakima were almost entirely geometrical; in later years stylized human and animal figures were introduced. The decorative designs of the Cowlitz baskets were identical in most respects with those of the Klickitat.

Baskets other than of round configuration were seldom made; by far the most common shape was that of an inverted, truncated cone. The Klickitat and the Yakima, like the Cowlitz, finish the rim coil with a false braid. In addition to the false braid some baskets had grass or root-wrapped loops around the rim edge. The attachment of loops or scallops was utilitarian, and if broken or worn, a new edge could be made more easily than a new solid coil finish.

Baskets were made for many purposes: storage, carrying loads, packing on horses, root gathering, berry picking and cooking. Nut-shaped baskets, similar to those of the Thompson, were used for storage or water jars.

Several kinds of woven baskets were made by the Klickitat, including a flexible type woven of Indian hemp or willow bark. Ornamentation was in false embroidery, with willow bark dyed black and tule in natural green or white colors or bear grass. These were also made in fairly large numbers by the Wasco, Wishram and Cowlitz.

The Nez Perce, the Wasco, the Umatilla, the Cayuse and other tribes east of the Cascades did not make stiff baskets. They were peoples who were much in the saddle and their baskets were essentially pouches, both round and flat, usually flexible and of strong, durable workmanship, making them suitable for use in transport.

Bear grass (Xerophyllum tenax)

The plateau area woven bags were twined of Indian hemp and ornamented with tule in its natural green, white and yellow colors. In early times ornamentation was applied in such a way as to wrap about or embrace the entire weft. The design created thus appeared on the inside of the bag as well as on the outside surface (total weft wrap). In later days, a false embroidery (external weft wrap) of corn husk and colored yarn was substituted for tule and willow bark. In this instance, the corn husk embraced the external element of the woven weft strands only and the design did not appear on the inside of the bag. Bags of this type were not manufactured by tribes living west of the Cascades.

Fez-shaped caps were woven and worn by the women of the Nez Perce; they were worn also by women of surrounding tribes as well as some west of the Cascades. Similar caps were also woven by the Klickitat.

The caps were woven of Indian hemp, ornamented with white or yellow-dyed bear grass or with natural or black willow. The application of the grass was over the entire surface and both elements of the weft were wrapped. In later times, they were made of corn husk and decorated with colored yarn.

Of all the Chinook tribes only the Wasco produced the distinctive style of basket or wallets, which are usually referred to as *sally bags*. These were cylindrical or pail-shaped, varied in height from a few inches to two feet, and made in plain twined weaving over a warp of hemp or rushes. The woven margins were frequently covered with a flexure of buckskin or fabric.

Patterns were made by overlaying, a total weft wrapping of the twined weave of hemp with strips of grass or corn husk. In later years the designs were pictorial representations of man, elk, sturgeon and duck, the stylized figures similar to some Columbia River pictographs and petroglyphs.

PUGET SOUND, HOOD CANAL, WASHINGTON COAST

The art of basketry in and around the Puget Sound region might be characterized not by a single type but by the great variation in types of baskets.

Communication and travel between the surrounding several tribes, the excellent work and patterns designed by some of these, and the more comfortable transportation and communication about the Sound, Hood Canal, and adjacent low lands perhaps explains the variety or mix of work.

There are plain checker weaving, twilled weaving of several types, coiling and imbrication and plain twined weaving in

Indian hemp (Apocynum cannabinum)

Klickitat type;
Coiling with imbrication

both open work and more tightly woven work. The various types are decorated with imbrication, occasionally with false embroidery, and with other overlay techniques which are an intimate part of the twining. It is evident there is a crossing over in the use of techniques between various geographic and linguistic groups.

Baskets from the Indians along the Skagit and Stillaguamish rivers and their tributaries are coiled, fairly even in surface contour, imbricated or beaded, with buckskin marginal carrying loops. They flare gently at the base and present modestly angular corners, suggesting the more northerly burden basket shape; yet, they are sufficiently oval to retain the suggestion of a more southern or eastern origin.

Indians in the area around the waterways of the Puyallup and Nisqually rivers produced both twined and coiled basketry. Checker weave baskets were also made, using cedar bark in a combination of black and natural color.

Three variations of twining were common, all reflecting variation in the tightness of the weave or the spacing of the warp and the weft elements. Twined baskets were made in various sizes for storage uses. Open-work clam baskets were also woven.

Coiled watertight baskets were used for stone boiling and cooking, and also for food-gathering and berry picking.

Although the coiled basket of the Cowlitz and those of the Puyallup-Nisqually region are difficult to differentiate, *Cowlitz-type* is the term applied to coiled basketry of much of western Washington, particularly the area of Puget Sound.

The Indians of the Cowlitz River district, it is said, produced the perfect coiled imbricated basket with more coils to the inch, more stitches and also more beauty in design.

Classically, the Cowlitz-type basket was finely coiled with a smooth, even wall. It was generally totally imbricated and finished with a braided rim, which embraced usually two loops of buckskin attached to a single side of the basket. The buckskin loops were used for the attachment of tumplines, the carrying strap worn over the bearer's head. Imbricated outlines were fashioned in wide vertical or diagonal bands, although geometrical patterns existed, such as zigzag configurations, bands including diamonds, chevrons or checker-shaped patterns. Human representations were occasionally used. Colors included brown, white, yellow and black combinations with occasionally a red or other color introduced.

Cedar roots, which grew along rotten logs, were long and straight and the preferred source of material for both foundation and sewing. For the imbrication, brown was usually sup-

Skokomish
Cattail and bear grass
plain twining with overlay double weft

Suquamish—cedar bark, bear grass, cedar root. Coiled basket with partial imbrication

19

plied by the cedar bark. Bear grass was used for white, for yellow after soaking for several days in a dye made from the inner bark of Oregon grape, for red after soaking in a dye made from the bark of alder. Red was also obtained from the bark of wild cherry. Black was occasionally made by immersing the grass in river mud, but a better material came from the roots of the bullrush, horsetail or watercress which was dug at a considerable depth. The white bast or inner bark of cedar was sometimes used and dyed yellow, red or black if the quantity of bear grass was not sufficient. This latter method was more frequently used by the Klickitat.

In general, the patterns of the Cowlitz-type coiled basket are less formal, not divided into fields or zones, and more consistently totally imbricated than the Thompson, Lillooet and Chilcotin. The Klickitat and Yakima baskets were, at times, decorated with dramatic eye-catching zigzag bands of solid color and with more frequent use of representational figures.

Of the soft, collapsible, twined embroidered wallets made by the several tribes in the region, including the Quinault and the Clallam, those of the Skokomish are generally considered the finest. Materials consisted of strips of cattail leaves or a mixture of the leaves with cedar bast for the warp and two twining wefts. The twining of the Skokomish basket made use of bear grass (white or yellow) and bark (brown and black) as the third weft element (overlay) to effect a uniform surface finish and design. The design most commonly used is a fairly formal geometric arrangement of rectangles vertically structured and connected, extending from the bottom to the top margin of the basket. Other configurations were used, such as horizontal bands or a zigzag design, the latter either horizontal or vertical. Skokomish and Puget Sound basket makers are noted for their use of a row of animal figure designs about the upper margin of a basket.

Twined basketry was also used by the Snoqualmie and the Snohomish in making the small hats worn by the women.

The Quinault twined basket was stiff, tightly woven, frequently of medium size, and nicely proportioned with gently curving sides. The overlay, a double weft twining, was frequently used in making simple decorated patterns of zigzag lines running vertically, horizontally or obliquely.

The techniques, materials, ornamentation and types of baskets created by the Indians of the Northwest Coast are as varied as their great region, yet they are similar in the magnificent quality and beauty which makes them works of art.

Wild cherry (Prunus emarginata)

Cattail (Typha latifolia)

Coiled storage basket woven by a Lillooet, British Columbia, Indian from cedar root, cherry bark and rush.

Lillooet storage unit with wrapped rim, lid and button;
collected in the 19th century. It is a prized member of
the extensive assemblage of Mr. and Mrs. Gene Zema.

22

Coiled basket with lid, photographed along the lower Fraser River in British Columbia. This is where it was likely produced by the Stalo Indians at the turn of the century.

Plain twined carrying bag woven by a member of the Umatilla tribe during the beginning years of the 20th century. The twined Indian hemp and corn husk overlay form this unique geometric pattern. It was photographed with slowly eroding petroglyph at Vantage, Washington.

Cedar root, bear grass and horsetail root work well to form zigzag design of storage unit by Salish Indian. Right: Coiled storage basket from Salish reservation in western Washington. Geometric design was created from horsetail root, bear grass, cedar root and bark.

Clam basket with "bird cage" woven pattern formed with cedar bough splints, root and bark by Salish and Wakashan Indians. Viewed along shore of Samish Bay.

Setting for storage baskets woven by member of Klamath tribe who gave river its name. Tule and porcupine quills were used in this plain twining technique.

Petroglyphs are a prompt reminder of the creative, talents of Indians along the shore near Cape Alava. Cedar roots and bear grass overlay were used for trimming these Quinault storage baskets. Location of find was Bay City, Washington in 1897, by James Wickersham.

Coiled storage basket collected in Wapato, made of bear grass, cedar bark and root, horsetail root. Salish, possibly Wenatchi or Skagit. Carved wooden mortar and spoon from the Centerville, Washington, area. Wasco/Wishram. Following page: Good craftsmanship and typical design using bear grass, cedar bark and root. Yakima or Klickitat.

Cedar root and bear grass overlay combined to form this pattern by Quinault Indians along upper reaches of river that bears their name. Preceding page: Beautiful rendering of twined "rattle top" storage basket by Tlingit Indian. Materials used were spruce root, grass and the maidenhair fern. Chosen from collection of Mr. and Mrs. Gene Zema.

Salish storage and cooking baskets woven with rush, tule, cedar bark and root, near the year 1850. Collected in the Grays Harbor area, they are from the Paul Smits collection. Pictured at Nisqually flats, Washington.

Fraser River Gorge and lichen growth renders contrast for burden baskets at Lillooet, British Columbia. Woven of cedar root and bark, rush and cherry bark in the 19th century by members of that Salish tribe.

Athabascan coiled storage basket at home along shore of Yukon River. Willow, natural and dyed, well suited for fit of lid and shape, created by skillful hands.

Ryegrass, silk or worsted fabric favored by the Aleut Indians for storage and fish baskets. Aleutian Islands, seldom void of fog, was the locale for these efforts.

Young child's berry basket coiled by member of Salish tribe of Western Washington, using cedar root, cherry bark, bear grass and horsetail root. These materials combined with carpet of moss along Nisqually River, appear to be quite compatible.

Flexibility of cedar bark is revealed in weaving of storage or carrying basket by member of Kwakiutl tribe. Viewed along ocean shore of Vancouver Island where they once resided.

Coiled basket given to James Wickersham in 1899
by Puyallup Indians, Tom Tom Milroy and a little
girl. Woven with cedar root and bark, bear grass and
horsetail root, it is pleasing, functional and durable.

The Aleut Indians were so capable they forced us to return to the Aleutian Islands for another peek at their rye grass craftsmanship, which is exceptional.

Willapa Bay is the perfect setting for this cattail, bear grass, wrapped crossed warp production. History dictates we credit member of Chehalis tribe.

Storage capacity of cedar bark basket is exceeded by bountiful harvest along the British Columbia coast. Woven by member of Kwakiutl tribe in ending years of 19th century.

Close-up clearly reveals the coiled technique and imbrication practiced by Puyallup Indians. It was made of cedar root and bark, horsetail root and bear grass.

An abundance of sea shells exceeded the limits of these storage baskets along a southeast Alaska beach. Tlingit Indians fashioned their aesthetic geometric figures using spruce root, maidenhair fern and grass.

Nootka Indians called British Columbia their home so it seemed appropriate to capture their efforts lying on the western shore of lower Vancouver Island. Hat and wallet were woven with cedar bark and grass, adorned with the painted designs.

Northern Idaho, home of the Nez Perce, was the setting for this mid 19th century creation. The storage wallet was made from Indian hemp decorated with corn husks, applied as a false embroidery or external weft wrap.

Imbricated zigzag design with braided rim was accomplished over cedar root coiling with cedar bark, bear grass and horsetail root. Made by a Salish tribe at the turn of the century near Willapa Bay, Washington.

Paintbrush, lupine leaves and fleabane form a rare
display on the floor of meadow in the Cascade Range.

Bountiful harvest along Hood Canal, near Skokomish Indian Reservation fills storage wallets woven by members of tribe at the turn of the century. Cattail, bark and bear grass were used to form these geometric figures, an overlay with double weft twining. Below: Woven by members of same tribe, using identical stock, to gain these pleasing angular creations on Skokomish River.

Coiled baskets woven with cedar root, bear grass and horsetail root, by Salish Indians in Nisqually-Puyallup region of Washington. Below: Burden baskets coiled by Salish Indians along lower Fraser River, in British Columbia. They combined cedar root, rush, cherry bark. The coils of the basket on the left were formed over cedar splints; on the right, over a bundle of split roots.

It was in this atmosphere that the various tribes of the northwest coast adapted their many crafts so well. The flowering dogwood, one of our most attractive flowering trees, can be seen in practically all western forest areas.

Section of sally bag by Wasco Indian using indian hemp, grass, corn husk and buckskin. Following page: A blaze of color created from merging of lupine and Indian paintbrush forms an eye-catching mass of alpine flora, Olympic Mountains.

A creative design in perfect harmony with grass along the Skagit River flats in northwest Washington. Woven around 1880 by a Salish Indian using cedar root and bark, bear grass and horsetail root. Preceding page: Overhead view of Makah storage basket clearly delineating faultless design and perfect circumference.

Fully imbricated storage basket woven by Si-a-gut, a Salish Indian near headwaters of Nisqually River, Washington. Collected by James Wickersham, 1899.

Southeast Alaska, always identified with the Tlingit Indian, was the setting for display of their early talents. Spruce root, grass and maidenhair fern formed these storage baskets woven in late 19th century.

Pattern design in tune with region along the ocean side of Vancouver Island, British Columbia. Woven by Makah or Nootka Indians using raffia and bear grass.

Ninstints Village in the Queen Charlotte Islands is the setting for this scene. Using spruce root, the Haida and Tlingit Indians delivered this superb workmanship.

Setting sun highlights Skokomish storage wallets along the shore of Hood Canal. Salish tribe used cattail, bark and bear grass for this effort.

Petroglyphs etched in rock near tip of Cape Alava south of Cape Flattery at the extreme northwest corner of State of Washington. Storage baskets were woven by Makah Indians. Following page: Mussels are far more prevalent than the few remaining examples of twining by the Tlingit Indians who resided in this southwest Alaska coastal region. Materials put to use were the spruce root, with maidenhair fern and grass forming a false embroidery overlay.

Checker weave mat made from cedar root by a Nootka Indian in late 19th century. Preceding page: Ivory carving is decoration for an Eskimo coiled trinket basket made of baleen. Example is number 403 made by "Omnik," Point Hope, Alaska.

Along west coast of Vancouver Island this Nootka totem pole appears to be looking viewer straight in the eye. This art form is most unique when you realize it was executed by the use of primitive tools.

Moisture-laden oak ferns and oxalis flourish in the dank world of the Quinault rain forest. Appealing feature of Olympic National Park in western Washington.

Tlingit Indian storage baskets nestled against a fallen
totem pole at the edge of Ninstints Village, in Queen
Charlotte Islands, British Columbia. Plain twining with
cedar bark and spruce root in the late 19th century.

Deterioration of totem poles in contrast with late 19th century Haida Indian basket reveals the value of protection and preservation. This example of twining from spruce root eyed on Anthony Island in Queen Charlotte chain, British Columbia.

Close-up detail from sally bag woven by a Wasco Indian. Using Indian hemp, corn husk and buckskin, the end result was an unusual art form.

Realistic figures on basket and sally bag appear in harmony with a petroglyph named Tsagaglalal, or "She Who Watches", at the long narrows on the Columbia River. Woven by members of Chinook Wasco tribe, working with buckskin, Indian hemp, bear grass and corn husk. The bowl accompanying the bags is carved from mountain sheep horn, by a Chinook artist.

Flexible carrying bag or corn husk bag of the Nez Perce Indians. The Indian hemp foundation is tastefully embellished with an overlay, an external weft wrap or false embroidery.

Coiled burden baskets photographed along the Chilcotin River, in British Columbia. The Chilcotin Indians made use of cedar root, rush, cherry bark, bird quill, willow rod or wire in the formation of unique shape.

These fez shaped hats made from Indian hemp, corn husk and wool fabric are another example of twining. While commonly attributed to the Nez Perce they were woven and worn by others of the plateau tribes.

Another example of work by the Nez Perce Indians. This carrying bag woven with Indian hemp, twine, corn husk, and colored yarn was collected near Yakima, Washington, and woven at turn of century.

It seemed appropriate that this carrying basket be viewed on land adjoining the Columbia River in Central Washington, near the Yakima Indian Reservation. It was member of this tribe using cedar root and bark, bear grass and horsetail root that composed this coiled unit.

The Klickitat Indians roamed this semi-arid region along the Columbia River. Made of cedar root, bark, horsetail root and bear grass, they were collected in the community of Wapato, Washington, and made circa 1900.

On the eastern slope of the Cascade Range lies the Yakima Indian Reservation, birthplace of these carrying baskets, made of cedar root, bear grass and horsetail root. The basket at left was found in White Swan, the other in Wapato, Washington. Following page: Corn husk bag from combination of Indian hemp, corn husk and colored yarn by the Nez Perce.

Many a leaf has fallen since these petroglyphs were etched along the Columbia River and a lesser number following the completion of this carrying basket found near Yakima, Washington. A member of the Klickitat or Yakima tribe using cedar root, bear grass and horsetail root was rewarded for this creation. Preceding page: Coiled construction by an Alaskan Eskimo. Made of grass and bark it was purchased along Kuskokwim River near Bethel, Alaska.

It was in this region of southwest Washington that the Salish Indians found suitable materials to make their baskets. Native to this area was cedar root and bark, bear grass and horsetail root which they used repeatedly to coil many storage baskets. Dried stems of Oregon grape were used as a source of yellow dye.

Open mesh basket with plain twined lid using one of more traditional basket materials, cedar bark, by a Tlingit Indian. Collected by Mr. and Mrs. Gene Zema.

Decorative techniques of imbrication and beading by the Lillooet Indians is shown in upper two-thirds of this basket. Viewed by Fraser River, British Columbia.

79

Age takes it toll when you compare the birch bark of today versus the bark of 100 years ago. This fragile appearing Athabascan Indian carrying basket was viewed near the Yukon River in the interior of Alaska.

Nestled among rocks along the Skagit River are examples of work quite possibly by the tribe that gave the river its identity. Cedar root, bear grass, cherry bark and rush, were employed to achieve this final result.

Evening sunlight accentuates the wrapped crossed warp technique of the Nootka and Makah Indians viewed along the ocean side of Vancouver Island, British Columbia near Clo-oose. This composition using cedar bark, bear grass and sedge grass had distinction of not being akin to any other tribe.

Clean lines of these storage baskets coincides with the shore line of the Puyallup River. Unit on the left was found at Oyster Bay in 1894 and the other at Clark's Corner, Washington in 1899. Following page: Wrapped crossed warp technique reveals desire for perfection by Makah Indian, at Neah Bay, Washington.

Resting on a ledge of the treeless, desolate Aleutian Islands is another example of some of the finest basketry in the world. These were woven with rye grass and decorated with a silk false embroidery. They were found on the island of Attu by Mr. Alan May while on a Smithsonian expedition. Preceding page: We did not count the contents, but the structure of this trinket basket woven with cedar root, bear grass and woolen yarn dictates durability. This effort by Klickitat Indian was found near The Dalles, Oregon.

The pliability of cedar root, rush and cherry bark is proven by the Salish tribes of British Columbia. Baby carrier, storage trunk, tobacco and pipe pouch were coiled by Lillooet and Thompson Indians in the late 19th century. Photographs taken along lower Fraser River, near town of Hope.

Coiled basket of bear grass, cedar root and bark, made at Silver Creek on upper Cowlitz River. Collected by James Wickersham, Mud Bay, Washington in 1899.

Upper Lewis River setting for this coiled basket by member of Salish tribe imbricated, with braided rim; made from cedar root, bear grass and horsetail root.

Coiled imbricated baskets by the Cowlitz and Lewis rivers, was site of manufacture by Salish Indians from cedar root, bark, bear grass, and horsetail root. Collected in 1900 at Kelso, Washington by Ford Carothers.

Buckskin suspension thongs and bent wood support for cloth sun-shade assist in the utilization of this baby carrier. Lillooet Indians relied on cedar root, and splints, with cherry bark and rush to decorate baskets.

"Sally bag" a distinctive style woven by the Wasco Indians. Note use of buckskin around rim of Indian hemp basket, with corn husk used to effect classic X-ray style decoration. Photographed at long narrows, on Upper Columbia River. Two old spoons from same general area complete the assemblage.

Haida Indian poles on Anthony Island in the Queen Charlotte chain reflect violent conditions that abrade their surface.

Vine maple and cottonwood leaves denote seasonal change on floor of the Yakima Indian Reservation, in foot-hills along eastern slope of the Cascade Range.

Summer sunset on Olympic Peninsula reveals exacting talent of Puyallup Indians. Storage baskets collected from Mrs. Chehalis Bill in 1899, by James Wickersham.

Clam baskets woven with cedar root and bark appear to be the same age as the weatherworn totem poles in remote area of the Queen Charlotte Islands, British Columbia.

An ancient basket from a significant collection makes an appearance in the Skagit River Valley. This finely coiled, totally imbricated work may well date to time of Wilkes expedition and exploration in southwest Washington.

Frost covered foliage in sharp contrast with youngsters berry basket and larger storage basket. Coiled of cedar root and bark, bear grass and horsetail root, both were eyed in the Yakima valley and formed by the Yakima or Klickitat peoples.

Hat and mat made solely of cedar bark by Nootka Indians. Perhaps same hand that painted the mat and hat also created the stark 19th century mask.

Woman's work basket with rattle top, formed by a Tlingit Indian from spruce root, grass, and maiden hair fern. In background is seen a section of Tlingit Chilkat blanket.

Along the mid-fork of the Snoqualmie River where the Salish tribes once roamed, is the setting for this coiled storage basket. Likely Lillooet in origin dating to late 19th century, it is made from cedar root, cherry bark and rush. Property of Mr. and Mrs. Gene Zema. Following page: Trio of plaited storage baskets by members of the Tsimshian tribe using their favorite fiber, cedar bark. They are now included in the permanent display at Burke Memorial Washington State Museum in Seattle.

Unusually fine trinket basket made of cedar bark, sedge and bear grass by Mrs. Schuyler Colfax, Makah Indian, at Neah Bay, Washington, early in the 20th century. Preceding page: Classic Lillooet basket, probably mid 19th century. Coiled with cedar root and decorated with cherry bark and rush.

Sunlight enters opening in dense foliage to define Salish tribe storage basket along the Skagit River. Coiled with cedar root and splints, bear grass and cherry bark, in late 19th century, and collected at Darrington, Washington.

Along the shore of Satus Creek, a one-time habitat of the Klickitat Indians, was the proper placement for this original work. Coiled with cedar root and bark, bear grass and horsetail root they were collected in Wapato, Washington and date to the turn of the century. Below: Burden baskets coiled by the Chilcotin Indians using cedar root, rush, cherry bark, bird quill and the willow rod. Their unique features include a curved margin, a four-field design and marginal circling rod or wire.

A grouping of coiled storage baskets exhibit the work of Salish Indians in British Columbia. These are Lower Fraser (Stalo), Thompson and Lillooet. Made from cedar root, rush and cherry bark, they were collected by E. A. Kipp in Chilliwack, British Columbia. Below: Cowlitz Indian baskets coiled with a smooth wall, imbricated, with a braided rim and fashioned from cedar root and bark, bear grass and horsetail root.

Logs in foreground arrived long after the Makah Indians wandered this northern coast of Washington. Sea stacks in background reveal the ruggedness of this region.

Deep in the rain forest of Olympic National Park, is this luxuriant region doused by average of 150 inches of rain each year.

Very old Salish storage and cooking baskets, coiled with cedar root and bark, bear grass, cherry bark and rush. Food was boiled by throwing hot stones into water-containing baskets. They are from the collection of the late Paul Smits and at one time graced a cozy summer home on the Southwest Washington coast.

107

Modern art forms cannot improve on the tasteful patterns woven by the Nez Perce. This "corn husk bag" or wallet was made of hemp, corn husk and dyed yarn.

Moss-laden area of the Olympic Mountain Range provides delightful corridor for the Quilcene River rolling eastward to merge with Hood Canal.

Petroglyph on face of narrows along Columbia River is in perfect harmony with the Wasco Indian sally bags. Indian hemp, corn husk, and buckskin were employed to form the traditional skeletonized or "X-ray" style.

Varied handiwork of the Nez Perce Indians is identified with two techniques. Overlaid twined wallet of
Indian hemp, corn husk and colored yarn is reflected
in the colorful blending of buckskin, beads and cloth.

Plain twining with cedar bark and grass was done by
Tsimshian Indians of British Columbia. Can be viewed
at Burke Memorial Washington State Museum, Seattle.

Melting snow gently spills over lichen-covered rocks on the western slope of Cascade Range.

Field of Indian paint-brush forms a sea of color along alpine trail, in the Olympic Mountains of northwest Washington.

Summit of Mt. Index rises abruptly from valley floor
along the Cascade Range, south of Skykomish River.

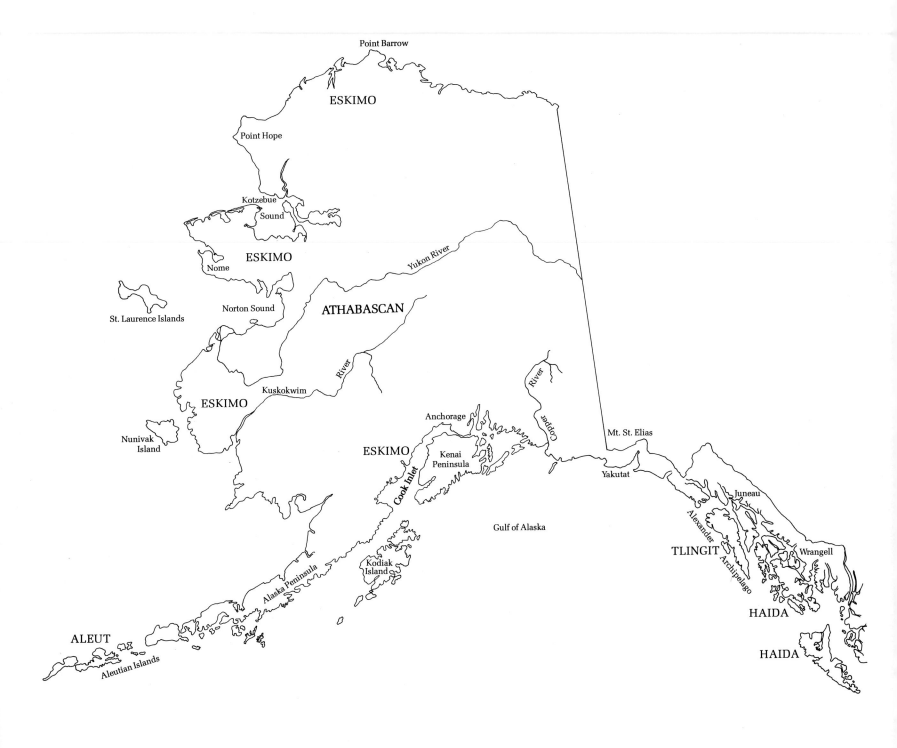

Point Barrow

ESKIMO

Point Hope

Kotzebue
Sound

ESKIMO

Nome

Yukon River

St. Laurence Islands

Norton Sound

ATHABASCAN

River

Kuskokwim

ESKIMO

Nunivak
Island

Anchorage

Copper River

Mt. St. Elias

Kenai
Peninsula

ESKIMO

Cook Inlet

Yakutat

Juneau

Gulf of Alaska

Alexander Archipelago

TLINGIT

Wrangell

Alaska Peninsula

Kodiak
Island

HAIDA

ALEUT

HAIDA

Aleutian Islands

TLINGIT

ATHABASCAN

Alexander Archipelago

TLINGIT

HAIDA

Nass *River*

River

TSIMSHIAN

Queen

Prince
Rupert

Skeena

HAIDA

Charlotte Islands

Prince George

BELLA
COOLA

KWAKIUTL

SHUSWAP

CHILCOTIN

Chilcotin

LILLOOET

Lillooet River

Fraser River

Thompson River

KWAKIUTL

COAST

THOMPSON

Vancouver Island

OKANOGAN

NOOTKA

STALO

SALISH

117

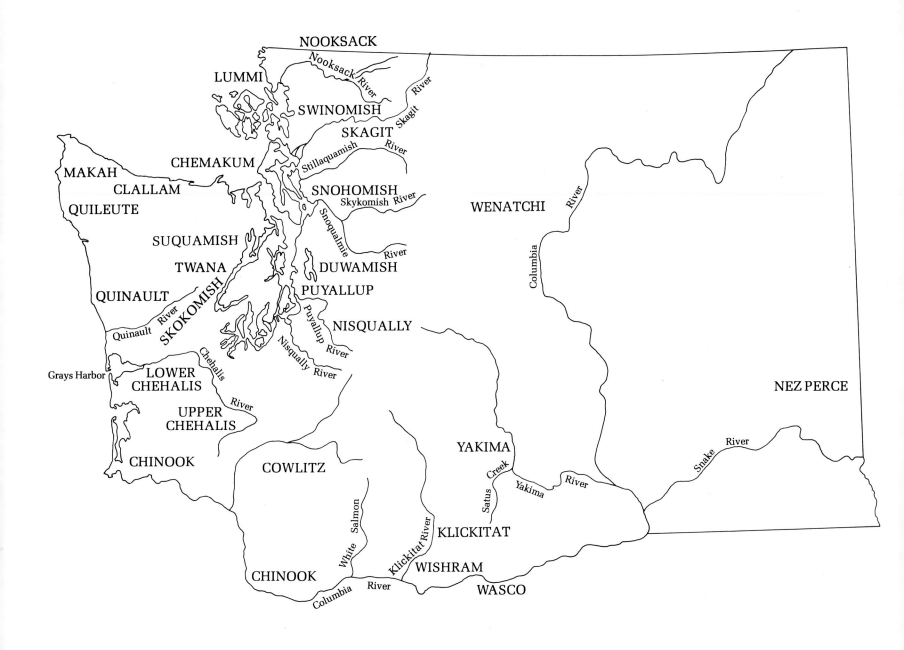

INDEX

BASKET DIMENSIONS

Page	Width and height (in.)	Centimeters	Page	Width and height (in.)	Centimeters	Page	Width and height (in.)	Centimeters	Page	Width and height (in.)	Centimeters
21	16½ x 12	(42 x 31)	45 (b)	10½ x 7½	(27 x 19)	69 (a)	9½ x 7½	(24 x 19)	92 (a)	15 x 12	(38 x 30.5)
22	13 x 7	(33 x 18)	46 upper (a)	5½ x 4½	(14 x 11)	69 (b)	14 x 11	(35 x 38)	92 (b)	10½ x 10½	(27 x 27)
23	7 x 5½	(19 x 15)	46 upper (b)	7 x 6	(18 x 15.5)	70 (a)	7 x 6½	(18 x 16.5)	92 (c)	14½ x 12	(37 x 30.5)
24	8 x 12	(20 x 31)	46 upper (c)	3 x 2½	(7 x 6)	70 (b)	6½ x 5½	(16.5 x 14)	93 (a)	16½ x 10½	(42 x 26)
25 left	10¼ x 10½	(26 x 27)	46 upper (d)	5½ x 4½	(14 x 11)	71	14 x 17	(35.5 x 43)	93 (b)	17 x 11	(43 x 27.5)
right	8½ x 7	(21.5 x 17.5)	47 lower (a)	15 x 13½	(39 x 34)	72	12 x 16	(30.5 x 41)	94	13 x 6½	(33 x 16.5)
26 left (a)	14½ x 11	(37 x 29)	47 lower (b)	16½ x 13½	(42 x 34)	73 (a)	13½ x 14½	(34 x 37.5)	95 (a)	11 x 10½	(27 x 27)
26 left (b)	12¾ x 8	(32 x 20)	48 upper (a)	8¼ x 5¼	(21 x 13)	73 (b)	12 x 13½	(30 x 34)	95 (b)	4 x 4	(10 x 10)
26 right (a)	4½ x 2½	(11 x 7)	48 upper (b)	6 x 4½	(15 x 11.5)	74 (a)	9½ x 10	(24 x 26)	96 (a)	56 x 36	(143 x 92)
26 right (b)	5½ x 3¾	(15 x 9.5)	48 lower (a)	14 x 9½	(35.5 x 24)	74 (b)	14 x 15½	(35 x 39)	96 (b)	12½ x 7	(32 x 18)
27 (a)	10½ x 10½	(17 x 17)	48 lower (b)	15½ x 9½	(39.5 x 24)	75	10 x 12	(25 x 30)	97	7½ x 5	(19 x 13)
27 (b)	9½ x 8	(24 x 20)	52	7¾ x 3½	(19.5 x 9)	76	9½ x 10	(24 x 26)	98	20½ x 6½	(52 x 17)
28	13½ x 14½	(34 x 37)	53	17 x 14½	(43 x 3)	77	13 x 15	(33 x 38)	99 (a)	6 x 4½	(15.5 x 11.5)
29	14 x 14	(35 x 35)	54	7 x 5½	(18 x 14)	78	9½ x 8	(24 x 20)	99 (b)	9 x 9¾	(23 x 25)
30	5½ x 4½	(14 x 11.5)	55 left (a)	7 x 5¼	(18 x 14)	79 left	7½ x 5½	(19 x 14)	99 (c)	6 x 4½	(15.5 x 11.5)
31	9½ x 7½	(24 x 19)	55 left (b)	4 x 4	(10 x 10)	79 right	16½ x 12	(42 x 30)	99 (d)	5¼ x 4	(13.5 x 10)
32 (a)	11 x 8½	(28 x 21.5)	55 right (a)	8 x 7¼	(20 x 18)	80 left	7 x 7	(17 x 17)	100	15½ x 11	(39 x 28)
32 (b)	14 x 11½	(35.5 x 29)	55 right (b)	11½ x 10½	(28 x 26)	80 right (a)	11 x 10	(27 x 25)	101	3 x 1¾	(8 x 4½)
33 left	19 x 14	(48 x 35.5)	56 left	4 x 5½	(10 x 14)	80 right (b)	14 x 14½	(36 x 37)	102	10 x 10	(25.5 x 25.5)
33 right	19 x 12½	(48 x 32)	56 right (a)	5 x 6	(12.5 x 15)	80 right (c)	8 x 5	(21 x 13)	103 upper (a)	16½ x 13½	(42 x 34)
34 left	14½ x 14½	(37 x 37)	56 right (b)	7 x 8	(18 x 20)	81	14	(35.5)	103 upper (b)	14 x 13½	(37 x 34)
34 right (a)	4 x 4½	(10 x 11.5)	57 (a)	6 x 4½	(15 x 11.5)	81 (b)	6½ x 3	(16.5 x 7.5)	103 lower (a)	9½ x 7½	(24 x 19)
34 right (b)	6½ x 7	(16.5 x 17.5)	57 (b)	7 x 6½	(18 x 16.5)	82 (a)	7½ x 4	(19 x 10)	103 lower (b)	14 x 12½	(35.5 x 32)
35	5½ x 5	(14 x 13)	57 (c)	13 x 14	(33 x 35.5)	82 (b)	11½ x 3½	(30 x 9)	104 upper (a)	11 x 7½	(28 x 19)
36	18 x 12	(46 x 30)	58 (a)	4 x 3½	(10 x 9)	83	7¾ x 3½	(20 x 9)	104 upper (b)	8½ x 4	(22 x 10)
37	12 x 3½	(21 x 9)	58 (b)	7¾ x 3½	(19.5 x 9)	84	5 x 3½	(13 x 9)	104 upper (c)	14½ x 4½	(37 x 11.5)
38 (a)	12 x 9	(30 x 23)	59 (a)	5½ x 4½	(14 x 11.5)	85 (a)	3¾ x 3¼	(9.5 x 8.5)	104 lower (a)	10½ x 7	(26 x 18)
38 (b)	6 x 6½	(15 x 16.5)	59 (b)	6 x 5½	(16 x 14)	85 (b)	3 x 3	(8 x 8)	104 lower (b)	6¾ x 5¼	(17 x 13)
38 (c)	3¾ x 4¼	(9.5 x 11)	60	4 x 3½	(10 x 9)	85 (c)	7 x 7	(18 x 18)	107 (a)	15 x 9	(38 x 23)
39	6½ x 3½	(16 x 9)	61	56 x 36	(143 x 92)	86 (a)	26 x 4½	(66 x 11.5)	107 (b)	19½ x 14	(50 x 36)
40	18 x 12	(46 x 30)	64 (a)	7½ x 6½	(19 x 16.5)	86 (b)	10½ x 8	(27 x 20)	108	10 x 12	(25 x 30.5)
42 (a)	5½ x 4½	(14 x 11.5)	64 (b)	5½ x 7	(14 x 18)	86 (c)	26 x 15½	(66 x 39)	110 (a)	7 x 11	(18 x 28)
42 (b)	3 x 2¼	(8 x 6)	64 (c)	7 x 8	(18 x 20)	87 left	11 x 9½	(28 x 24)	110 (b)	7½ x 11	(19 x 28)
42 (c)	3½ x 3¾	(9 x 10)	65	5 x 6	(12.5 x 15)	87 right	14½ x 12	(37 x 30.5)	111 (a)	6 x 6½	(15 x 16.5)
43 (a)	17 x 10	(43 x 24)	67 (a)	6 x 5¾	(16 x 14.5)	88 left (a)	7½ x 6½	(19 x 16.5)	111 (b)	7 x 8	(18 x 20)
43 (b)	13 x 6¾	(33 x 17)	67 (b)	7 x 11	(18 x 27)	88 left (b)	6¾ x 6¼	(17 x 16)	112 (a)	7 x 5½	(18 x 14)
44	22 x 29	(55 x 72)	68 (a)	15½ x 21	(39 x 54)	88 right	26 x 4½	(66 x 11.5)	112 (b)	6½ x 4½	(16.5 x 11.5
45 (a)	9½ x 9	(24 x 23)	68 (b)	12 x 15	(30 x 39)	89	6½ x 9½	(16 x 24)			